Monkey Business

UNIT 3

By Marilyn Sprick

Illustrated by Larry Nolte

Main Characters

Who is this? (Mo)

Who is this? (Max)

Vocabulary Words

zoo

zookeeper

cab

Table of Contents

STORY 1, DUET

Chapter 1, Mo 1

Mo, the monkey, lives in the zoo.

STORY 2, SOLO

Chapter 2, 1 5

See one monkey. See Mo.

STORY 3, DUET

Chapter 3, Sad Mo 6

Max takes Mo to town, hoping to make her happy.

STORY 4, SOLO

Chapter 4, See Me! 9

I see me.

STORY 5, DUET

Chapter 5, Max and Mo 10

Max and Mo go to the restaurant.

STORY 6, SOLO

Chapter 6, I'm 14

I'm happy.

DUET STORIES: Adults read the small text. Students read the large text.

Monkey Business

CHAPTER I • MO

This is Mo.

Put your finger on the dot under Mo. Who is the story about? (Mo)

Say hello to little Mo. (Hello, Mo.)

Where do you think Mo lives?

See I .

See one little monkey who lives in the zoo.

Where does Mo live? (In the zoo)

This is Max.

Put your finger on the dot under Max.

Say hello to Max. (Hello, Max.)

Where do you think Max works?

See  .

Max is the zookeeper. Max works at the zoo.

These are the children who visit the zoo.

The children look at Mo, and Mo looks back.

The children wave at Mo, and Mo waves back.

Everyone, wave at Mo.

 see. Monkey do.

The children love visiting Mo because Mo does whatever she sees the children do.

Monkey see. Monkey do.

When the children wave, what does Mo do then? (Mo waves back.)

Everyone, wave at Mo.

Max, the zookeeper, takes care of the animals. One day Max said, "Mo, you seem sad. Are you sick?" Mo shook her head.

Everyone shake your head.

Was Mo sick? (No)

What was the problem? (She seemed sad.)

"Ee, ee, ee."
• • •

Max said to Mo, "You seem sad. I think I know just what you need."

What's the problem? (Mo seems sad.)

What do you think Max will do?

CHAPTER 2

•   •

Who is the story about? (1 monkey)

See I  .

•   •   •

See  .

•   •

I see I  .

•   •   •   •

I see  .

•   •   •

How many monkeys do you see? (1)

Who is the monkey? (Mo)

CHAPTER 3

Sad Mo

One day Mo said,

"Ee, ee, ee."

Max, the zookeeper, said, "Poor little Mo. You seem sad. I think you must be bored! I know just the thing for you."

What's the problem? (Mo seems sad.)

What do you think Max will do?

With that, Max took Mo on a trip to the city. Their first stop was the gym.

Weight-lifting class was just about to begin. Someone handed Mo some gym clothes and a set of weights.

Where did Max take Mo? (To the gym)

Mo learned to lift weights. She smiled and seemed to say,

"See me. See me."

•   •   •   •

Do you think Mo is having fun?

By the end of class, Mo could lift a 20-pound weight.

Everyone clapped for Mo.

•   •   •   •

What could Mo do? (Lift a 20-pound weight)

Their next stop was a ballet studio. Someone handed Mo a leotard and ballet shoes.

What do you think Mo will learn to do?

Mo learned to stretch and do an arabesque. Mo seemed to say,

"See me. See me."

● ● ● ●

What did Mo learn? (How to stretch and do an arabesque)

Look at the picture. Everyone, stretch just like Mo.

By the end of class, Mo could perform an arabesque. Everyone clapped and said,

"See . See ."

● ● ● ●

CHAPTER 4

See Me

What's the title of the story? (See Me!)

See me.

See me.

I see me.

I'm 🙂.

Who is in the mirror? (Mo)

How does she feel? (Happy)

CHAPTER 5

Max and Mo

Max took Mo to a weight-lifting class and then to a ballet class. Mo had a grand time, but as soon as class was over, she seemed sad again. Max was surprised. Then Max looked at his watch. "I know just what you need," said Max.

What do you think the problem was?

See . See .

See I .

Where do you think Max is taking Mo?

Soon the cab pulled up in front of the best restaurant in the city. Smells drifted to the street. Mo looked happy. Mo said,

"Mmm, mmm, mmm."
  •   •   •

Someone handed Mo a lace shawl and a flowered hat, and soon Max and Mo were seated.

See .
  •   •

Where did Max take Mo? (To a restaurant)

Mo sat quietly at the table, but you could almost hear her say,

"See me. See me."

● ● ● ●

Mo looked grand.

Do you think Mo was having a fun time?

When Max looked at the menu, Mo looked at the menu.

When Max put a napkin on his lap, Mo put a napkin on her lap.

The waiter was impressed! What a polite little monkey.

Max and Mo had a fine feast, but Mo seemed sad. Max said, "I know just what you need." With that, Mo and Max climbed back in the cab.

Where do you think they're going now?

Soon Max and Mo were back at the zoo. Mo clapped her hands and climbed up in her tree on the little island in the middle of the zoo. Mo was tired and happy to be at home. Soon Mo was sound asleep.

Why was Mo happy to be home? (She was tired.)

The next day, the children came to visit. Mo waved and the children waved back.

"Mo is happy," thought Max. "I think we'll stay home today."

Was Mo glad to be back at the zoo?

CHAPTER 6

I'm

• •

Who is the story about? (Mo)

I'm .

• •

See me.

• •

See me.

• •

See me.

• •

I'm .

• •

Look at the pictures.

What are three things that make Mo happy? (Weight lifting, ballet, and waving to the children)